BEHAVE LIKE A STARTUP

First printed by:
RR Donnelley
4101 Winfield Road
Warrenville, IL 60555

Contact Ross Shafer
www.RossShafer.com

ISBN: 978-0-9975336-1-3

Printed in the United States of America
Cover and text design by *the*BookDesigners

THE CURE FOR CREEPING COMPLACENCY

BEHAVE LIKE A

STARTUP

ROSS SHAFER

INTRODUCTION

Are You Still Celebrating Yesterday's Success?

If you have been part of a company that has been wildly successful, then you are to be congratulated.

That said, if you've had such a prolonged run of good fortune, is it possible your organization is no longer "hungry?" Do you find that you are not as reactive as you once were? Have you noticed that your team is taking shortcuts instead of performing at your normal world-class thoroughness? Is it possible that you are still celebrating yesterday's profits while your competitors are revealing breakthroughs and innovations?

Maybe it's Time to Learn from the Start-Up Mentality?

Start-ups do not suffer from a lack of hunger. They have an unmistakable energy. Teamwork, in a Start-up, is fueled by a sense of mission and ownership in new ideas. Start-ups make bold decisions because they aren't yet at the point of risking long-term relationships. Marketing and staff budgets are necessarily skinny so they have to accomplish a lot...with a little. With scarce time or resources to make perfect products (or refine services), they frequently launch in Beta Mode because speed-to-market is so critical. They are not intimidated by larger companies because they believe they can offer something the "Big Dogs" cannot. The rub for a legacy organization is that soon you will be competing with a Start-up. Therefore you could benefit from being more nimble, more urgent, more flexible, reasonably open to risk, and willing to change tactics more quickly when market conditions shift beneath your feet.

Create the Start-Up Buzz, Again

Remember when your organization got write-ups in the trade papers? Do you recall when customers came to you by way of a personal recommendation? You were the "next big thing" and that attention was called "buzz."

Now the Start-ups are creating the "buzz" because they are fearless in their pursuit of gaining credibility and unique offerings. They disrupt the market in an attempt to turn the attention to themselves. In a high velocity recommendation economy, "buzz" is important to your clients and customers. Such popularity stamps you with the "hot" seal of approval; which helps your clients/customers/members to believe they are partnering with an entity that will get them to the future first.

There Really is a Cure for Complacency

I know it's a big promise packed into a little book. Unfortunately, it won't happen overnight, but you can do it. So, if you're willing to invest a little time, let's go get your mojo back!

CONTENTS

CHAPTER 1

IS COMPLACENCY CREEPING IN?

What Causes Complacency?

Usually it's when you have been making too much money.

Complacency can slowly creep in when everything is going too well. You've grown your market share. You've garnered respect in your industry. Your customers have loved you for a long time. You've hired a lot of talented people. In fact, you were probably a groundbreaker when you started but as time went on new ideas gave way to burgeoning profits. Your energy and focus was poured into aligning your core competencies. Your team wrote mission statements and a code of ethics designed to protect your brand, your market share, and preserve the value proposition of your beloved products or services. All good things... until your once great way of doing business just wasn't good enough anymore. Other players have begun to erode your margins and market share.

What Does Complacency Look Like?

Complacency manifests itself when your processes aren't as thorough as they used to be. Maybe you developed a successful six-step formula for digging up leads and closing sales, but you now find that some of those steps are being jumped over in the interest of "making life easier" or closing the sale more quickly. You will start to hear your team members assign blame and make excuses about everything from rumors - to government regulation - to a competitor's malpractice.

Maybe your client cold call volume has been going down and nobody is doing anything about it. Maybe your sales and marketing teams have been asking for new CRM or social-listening technology while senior leaders pour money into other non-revenue producing projects. Your customer complaints are up because your team members don't nurture relationships like they used to. You became so giddy about acquisition opportunities that some of the best senior leaders were syphoned off to run the new companies, leaving core responsibilities to inadequately trained team members.

If any of this sounds familiar, your success may have seduced you into thinking your market-leading position was invincible. You can imagine how much swaggering must have taken place at RIM in 2006 (creator of the Blackberry phones) before the iPhone was introduced a year later and decimated RIM's market share.

Complacency by Burnout

When tensions are high because (1) You want to push your company to world domination or (2) You are panicked because you are losing market share, there is a tendency for leaders to put more pressure on the team with questions like,

"How close are we to winning it all?"

"Who is taking their foot off the accelerator around here?"

"Why are we getting our lunch eaten by XYZ Company?"

Does getting angry with (or shaming) people motivate them to work harder?

Nope.

If you keep cracking the whip in an already tense work environment, you are whipping up a recipe for burnout. Good people get exhausted from pushing the ball uphill so hard (and for so long). Extreme pressure causes people to start making dumb mistakes. They start arguments at work. They go home early. They call in sick. They have no interest in trying something new. And when people are burned out, they push back. With complacency, pressure, and burnout the result is often a team that is simply not engaged anymore.

Long Periods of Uncertainty

Rumors begin circulating about a buyout or that key people are being replaced fuel complacency. Certain business units start to break off to support different ideas. Unshakable team members drop the ball more often than usual; especially when there isn't a balance of joy in the work. Further, if you want to stab your hard working team in the heart and twist the knife, tell them, "You need to start thinking and acting like an owner." That is a brutally insulting tactic particularly if they know they are not getting paid like an owner.

Did You Cause the Complacency?

Maybe you aren't getting full performance out of your team because leadership keeps complaining about government regulation killing the business; which causes insecurity. Or, you have initiated a wave of outsourcing that scares people into hiding. Those kinds of distractions (real or not) are a cancer in an organization.

Those distractions don't plague the Start-up. The Start-up is trying to make everybody feel important because the team is focusing on victory not victim-hood.

What is the Worst Kind of Complacency?

Disengaged Obstructionists.

People in burnout can slow down the workflows in an effort to make everything move at their pace. Regulating the speed and productivity of the processes is the only thing they feel they can control.

Complacency that turns into disengagement can destroy you.

Some obstructionists become territorial and will either hoard the information that affects progress, or find reasons to slow down the process. I have one friend who manages twelve extremely brilliant software engineers. Because they are constantly swamped to deliver tomorrow's technology (by yesterday), they are not interested in looking for ways to improve performance. They think if they just do what's required, management will have no room to complain. In one instance, my friend noticed the primary e-commerce App wasn't auto-populating the customer's name, address, and state on the order form. The conversation with the software engineer went like this:

MGR: Danny, did you notice the auto-populate feature was broken?"

DANNY: Yes, I did.

MGR: Man, why didn't you go in and fix it?

DANNY: Nobody told me to.

In Business, There is No Autopilot.

Autopilots may work for airplanes, but not for your company. The greatest danger in putting your company on autopilot is expecting that business will just show up whenever you snap your fingers. Autopilot assumes that you're operating an organization solely from your perspective. Autopilot-ing does not respect what your fickle customers and clients want from you; tomorrow.

Sometimes complacency surfaces as being downright lazy about achieving new goals. Watch what happens when leaders create outrageous goals that are simply not practical anymore. I spoke for one Fortune 100 company where the Chief Operating Officer stood at a podium and commanded the sales force to raise their sales target by 17%. He bellowed, "I know each and every one of you and I know you can do this!" I saw nothing but blank looks on the sales team's faces.

Then, the grumbling started.

One woman muttered to her seat mate, "He wants 17%? Exactly how does he think that's going to happen? We don't have any new products and he doesn't have a plan. This is insanity. I'm out."

Tight Company Policies Can Encourage Complacency

Over time, organizations that have become complacent, are usually rife with complex policies. They have written, published and built a long list of rules that may or may not be relevant anymore. If such policies were written a generation ago, do your policies conflict with the way people work today? For example, if you are a work-from-anywhere organization do your old policies still fit? Remember, policies must be relevant enough to adapt to current productivity and market shifts or your team will dismiss you. Are your policies flexible enough to encourage new ideas, or are your boundaries so tight that creativity has no place to thrive?

What are your policies with regard to onboarding new people? Could they be streamlined so that new team members can get up to speed more quickly?

Leadership Out-of-Focus Can Cause Mistrust

As a leader, it is your responsibility to make sure your organization is still living and breathing the mission and core values re: who you said you were. Are you inconsistent with the internal brand promises you made? Are you a self-starter who gives clear direction? How do you react in a morally-confusing situation? How do you handle unforeseen adversity? Is it possible that you were perceived as unfair in a previous crisis? Would you consider yourself accomplished, self-confident, and full of swagger? I suppose you can tell from the way I asked those questions that the opposite is how to keep people engaged. As a leader, you must be calm during a confusing situation. You must have a Plan A, a Plan B, and a Plan C, depending on the reality of your circumstances. You are expected to handle all manner of adversity and provide leadership that makes people feel they are in safe hands. At no time should you be considered unfair. That is not to say you can't be tough. But you must remain equitable in assigning responsibilities and course corrections. If anybody on your team feels you've dealt with them unfairly, the path back to re-engaging that person may take more time than you have. Look, I have nothing against self-confidence or swagger, but both are trumped by humility.

Complacency Must Die a Quick Death

There is no room in an organization for blame, making excuses, constant-complaining, useless-whining, under-the-breath grumbling, or sabotaging progress. The world is in constant flux. Markets change. Ideas and best practices are moving targets. So what you did in the past will eventually need refreshing. Too often "sticking with what worked" becomes an exercise in denial. We must be ever vigilant about what's next.

I love that we have a term in our economy called "trending" because now we have the advantages of big data and social-listening to adjust to what our customers expect from us, and how they like to buy.

CHAPTER 2

HOW DO STARTUPS BEHAVE?

If you've ever been part of an early Start-up organization, you know how exciting it was; especially when your challenge was to take business away from the market leader. There was probably a pot full of "group ownership" in the concept. Enthusiastic participation is natural because everyone is emotionally invested. If you remember, everyone bought-in psychologically because the entity was likely to be teetering on financial ruin. (Many of you may have even mortgaged your homes).

Admire the Energy of a Start-Up

Risks aside, a Start-up has an organic energy to it. If you've ever visited a Start-up office, you noticed that people were louder when they talked. They laughed more. There was camaraderie. Team members got together outside of work and were usually friends.

The vibe of a Start-up creates an exciting atmosphere because there isn't excess money flying around. As you can imagine, buckets of money is going out and not much coming in; which creates a feeling one start-up described as, "We fly or die together." The Start-up engine is driven by a mission to do something cool and potentially huge. The founder/leaders are 24/7/365 consumed by the mission. You might find a ping pong table or dartboard in the bullpen (bullpen = large open space designed for maximum collaboration). There are regular weekly parties and people are happy to swap schedules or sub for each other. Dress codes are loose and the offices are often dilapidated; replete with used furniture. Nobody cares. Shooting Nerf balls into hoops during a brainstorming session is a way to spark ingenuity. People talk about their relationships and hobbies without worry of judgement or recrimination. Team building may include common interests like fantasy football or sharing favorite YouTube videos. You would likely hear nicknames bandied about...born from the way a team member behaved during a meeting or phone call. The easiest nickname is your name and the letters STER or INATOR. The Nickster or the Bradster. I heard one young woman referred to as the Debinator because she was particularly lethal with arrogant techies. These nicknames aren't hatched from disrespect. Rather,they are a badge of honor, bestowed to valuable members of the team.

Yet despite the relaxed environment, everybody feels a sense of corporate social responsibility. The want to build a kickass company but they also want to do good for the world.

Quick Reactions. Less Bureaucracy.

In a Start-up, reaction time to solve problems is often instantaneous. Most times the Start-up is operating more on predictive analysis than historical forensics (because they have no historical analytics yet). They will scour the news and use every kind of business intelligence and social-listening software to expose a competitor's blind spots. What they lack in money, they make up for in enthusiasm and swift action. Everyone has multiple jobs and wouldn't dare print business cards because duties and responsibilities morph so quickly. Want to talk to the CEO? Not a problem. He or she might be acting as the receptionist when you call.

ZAPPOS: Don't Let a Wealthy Start-up Fool You

As a Start-up ZAPPOS had an advantage. The founder, Tony Hsieh, was only 24 when he sold his first company to Microsoft for $265 million. Surprisingly, that kind of wealth has no affect on the vibe you feel when you visit their building in Las Vegas, Nevada. The place reeks of entrepreneurialism. Tony sits in the middle of the giant room surrounded by cubicles that are individually decorated by the occupant. As a team member you might get a notice to join a 3 a.m. white board discussion. Harsh? No. You go because ZAPPOS makes you feel valued. Dedication to improving the customer's experience is tantamount to everything they do. They talk longer on the phone with customers than "professional call center consultants" say you should. If you don't fit the ZAPPOS culture, they might offer you a $5,000 quitting bonus. Stressed during the day? Why not slip into one of the Nap Rooms for a 20-minute power snooze. Though funded well, this start-up is not a glossy, staid culture. Their credo is to create fun and a little weirdness. Funny enough, one of the questions on their employment application is, "On a scale of 1-10, how weird are you?" In his autobiography, "Delivering Happiness" Tony Hsieh described the cultural evolution of his first big company (LinkExchange) and why he vowed to never let that happen at ZAPPOS. (paraphrasing) "Too many people were motivated by money and short-term reward. Too few were having fun. Going to work had become a drag. It was like death by a thousand paper cuts."

Has his weird, loose management style been productive? Apparently it has. ZAPPOS went from zero sales in 1999 to over $2 billion last year.

How Did Your Start-up Become Complacent?

Almost all Start-Ups are born lean. Their path to success typically focused on one or two prime directives. Deadlines were make-or-break critical as you worked your way toward the first big order. You were small enough that extreme accountability mattered. Expectations had to be met. And you still knew your people on a personal level. You knew their strengths and their idiosyncrasies. As a necessity, you measured your success daily, weekly, monthly, and quarterly. You may have even posted a salesperson "leaderboard" to track friendly competition. There was very little (if any) waste. Every person had a specific contribution to the effort.

If you were lucky enough to survive and grow into a mature company, you weren't as desperate so you started to define (and refine) the duties and responsibilities of each job. Because the lean days were now distant, you allowed long term loyalty as an excuse to keep on marginal performers. It's hard to let people go whom you've brainstormed with in those early all-nighter sessions. But as the company grew (and aged), more and more of the first people are unable to keep up. Rules become more flexible. Complacency creeps in. You can tell you are losing your mojo.

NOTE: Mojo is defined as a charm or talisman that is able to persuade others. I want you to resurrect the charm you once had to convince people to buy from you.

CHAPTER 3

PARTNERING WITH A START-UP

With some regularity, legacy companies see the value of buying Start-ups. Wall Street loves to see this because it makes the legacy company look cool. The perception is that a well-funded legacy company wants to hold hands with a younger culture so they can both skip into the future of innovation. Start-ups are sexy. And the partnership looks good on paper.

But if you're in the business of pleasing stockholders, be

careful. Growth has to be your top priority and melding a Start-up with your company could cause a severe culture clash. You may say to the Start-up, "We are experts at doing A, B, and C… but we need you to advise us on how to penetrate the market with X, Y and Z." It sounds like creating the perfect economic storm but it's worth reviewing the disastrous Time Warner AOL merger.

Media giant Time Warner was looking for a way to transition into the digital age. AOL was the leader in capturing tens of millions of new subscribers who wanted access to the Internet. Merging the two companies was to be a world-beating advertising coup.

Because AOL's valuation (in 1999) eclipsed that of Time Warner's, the deal would balloon to about $350 billion by January of 2000. Four months later, the Dot Com bubble burst and advertising slowed to the point that AOL could not meet it's financial forecasts. AOL's valuation would crash from $250 billion to roughly $20 billion by the end of the 2002.

What went wrong?

AOL grew very quickly due to its pervasive dial-up service. (Remember, there was no Google at that time, so AOL was the only way to jump into the net). But when the world demanded (and got) high-speed broadband Internet, AOL followed the extinction path of dinosaurs.

Further, neither company had thought through how to get paid for Internet-delivered content. Like many Dot Coms, the income projections were predicated on AOL's best guess, not reality. Finally, the two cultures just didn't get along. The generational divide was vast and neither company made a strong enough effort to learn and speak each other's language.

In the end, media mogul Ted Turner was probably the biggest loser. It is estimated that Turner lost approximately $8 billion in the process. Enthusiasm for a solid "old school" company to catch "the next big wave" turned into one of the most catastrophic merger deals of the last 50 years.

Due Diligence

That's not to say that you shouldn't consider partnering with a Start-up. Business schools now study the AOL/TIME WARNER kinds of debacles and today we know how to manage expectations and perform due diligence.

It can be a great marriage. As a legacy company, you bring stability and a checkbook. The Start-up brings progressive ideas and innovation. Since Start-ups are eager to win, by partnering with you there's no waiting to get access to important clients. As a legacy company, you have the resources to weather a slow start for any young company.

So, how do you leverage each other's strengths to enhance your mutual value propositions? Introduce your new partners to your long-standing clients. Let them tell their great stories of scaling and growth. You'll get the adulation for being innovative enough to partner with them. Think "Shark Tank" or "The Prophet" and remember that Start-ups want to connect with you for distribution, research and development, a safe harbor, and mentoring. Learn from the Start-up how they have accomplished so much in such a little time. Get them to explain (and execute) digital marketing for you. Learn how they collected and manipulated big data in order to grow so quickly. Introduce the Start-up to your other divisions for the purpose of accelerating scale. Be intentional about how you marry the two cultures. Work together on some of your easier projects so that you can see how the Start-up manages costs and resources. My suggestion would be to combine the sales and service entities because those are the areas that yield the quickest financial return. Be transparent about sharing information; which will also speed up the learning curve. Invite each other to give presentations to the respective teams so you can teach each other what it is you do. Questions and answer sessions are crucial as you both learn to live together.

Fewer Meetings. More Work.

Keep in mind that Start-ups meet fewer times a week and keep the meetings short. It's no joke that attention spans are declining and Start-ups would rather work than talk. So it's important to assign a liaison person in the Legacy company who can communicate with a similar-tiered person in the Start-up. If both are skilled communicators, they will grease the wheels quickly and it's always better to have one or two people as your "go to" partners.

CHAPTER 4

REGAINING YOUR MOJO

Going Back to the Future of Our Company

If you want to revive a start-up mentality in your legacy organization you might try being brave enough to call a meeting and ask your team questions other companies might be too afraid to ask.

What services can we provide that would render our competitors obsolete?

What unmet needs are we failing to fill?
If we started our business today, how would we attract customers?

How are we enticing the best people to join our team?

Are we paying for our employees to continue training and learning?

Are we still considered a truly great place to work?

Is there plenty of room for individual growth here?

Are we fairly rewarding the best decision-makers?

If you don't want to call a meeting, how about sending that list to your key folks and ask for their opinions. You might be surprised how many people would write back with, "It's about time someone asked those questions.

Signs of Complacency

First rule is this, don't try to run a business in denial. Pay acute attention to the overall mood of your company culture. You can tell your team is drifting into complacency when you notice these behaviors:

- They roll their eyes at new company initiatives. It's as if they are saying, "Yeah right, like that's going to happen." Your team is losing faith in your ability to execute new ideas.

- Casual Friday has leaked into Monday, Tuesday, and Wednesday. Coming to work too casual is a sign that people don't care...or that they are challenging your generosity.

- Team members stop rocking the boat; even when bad ideas are presented. If you have ever tiptoed through a marriage or love relationship because you feared rocking the boat, it means that you no longer feel safe with that person. The same is true at work. If you are afraid to voice an opinion for fear of repercussions, work is no longer a safe place and creativity evaporates.

- Collaboration has ground to a halt as "silos" have

built impenetrable walls to keep ideas and actions isolated from the rest of the company.

- Goals are picked apart with blame, excuses, and distractions.

- Company meetings include too many discussions of people who say, "I'd like to play devil's advocate on that idea."

- You find that you are spending a lot of time explaining to team members how inappropriate their social media postings have become. You don't want to police every employee's tweets or posts but you should make everyone aware of your social media code of conduct. The right posts can build an employee's personal brand. The wrong post can be devastating to the company. It is up to you to teach them the difference.

- People stop taking classes or seminars to improve their skills. It is a sign they have lost their drive to grow as a top performers.

- Company networking events are slowly losing attendance.

Short Cuts Rob Your Power

People who take the liberty of curtailing a successful process have decided not to be as diligent and detailed as they once were. Some might even believe that their solid track record gives them permission to circumvent the entirety of a process. It is important for you not to grant anybody permission to be lazy, regardless of experience or expertise. Laziness and taking short cuts can cause debilitating delays. Crucial errors and miscommunications could have been prevented had the abuser just stayed on course. Worse, hiccups in a proven process, due to a missed step, will not offer your best chance to compete in an urgent, on-demand economy. Hijacking a proven process with short cuts ignores what got you here in the first place.

Therefore, if you have a reliable, tactical process for success, then to be successful, (1) Do the job correctly every time and (2) Do the job so well that you consistently turn in a world-class performance.

For example: If a salesperson makes 25 cold calls each day, that salesperson will close a certain percentage of new customers. If the cold call process has 10 steps, and they are executed in the correct order, a new sale will be the result.

If you haven't had time to analyze what makes your company successful or train your staff with your time-tested methods for success, then take the time to create your successful sales process.

Accelerate Your Speed to Market

Having made a case for following the proven process model, there are times when you must rewrite the process to suit a changing market. You will know it's time to rewrite your process when your "proven" model is not producing the same percentage of predictable results. We live in a world of launching in Beta mode because we need customers and clients to tell us what's right and what's wrong. We all experience this with our smart device apps that are constantly being updated.

Don't Assume You Have Solid Relationships

Legacy companies sometimes assume that they've built such strong and lasting client relationships that they don't have to work as hard. But unless you remain vigilant, a start-up can swoop in with a fresh idea and land one of your best clients. Magnusson/Klemencic

Structural Engineering is a 93-year-old company that has designed and built some of the world's most recognizable buildings. Yet, their philosophy is: "We have an active data base of over 5,000 clients. We think of them as our friends. However, when we do a new pitch we send in the A-Team and act like it's our first time. We may win on our past work but we prefer to win on our enthusiasm."

Don't Allow Your Competitors to Surprise You

We never want to get caught with our market advantages down. So we must always know what our competitors are up to.

You may have sophisticated social listening software or B.I. (Business intelligence) programs. That's smart. But don't overlook the open sources. There is no excuse for you to be under-informed about who is vying for your dollars. Study your competitor's Twitter account. Join their Faccbook page. Do they Instagram? Are they on Tumblr? Subscribe to their RSS feeds. Sign up to get their press releases. Do they post YouTube videos? Do their customers add comments to their online "forum?" What about their public or private commercials or infomercials? Do they post them on YouTube or Vimeo? Somebody on your team should be reading the dozens of industry-specific blogs that comment on - or review your competition. All this is necessary if you don't want to be blindsided by an innovation. You don't want to read about an inventive, new practice that could have been instrumental in growing your business. Incidentally, you should expect that your competition is using the same tactics to study you and your organization.

Appoint a Chief Trending Officer

One technique we insist our clients practice is the habit of appointing a "Chief Trending Officer" for every meeting. This is not an official title or even a paid position but here is why it can be so valuable. Next time you have a meeting, charge someone with the duty of apprising you of new trends. Have this person do a five-minute oral report on relevant news items in your industry. Have them address rumors they've heard from friends or colleagues. The only rule is, "teach us something we don't already know."

You will be surprised by what your de-facto CTO will bring to the next meeting.

Generate More Ideas Than a Start-Up

You should be able to pull this off easily. After all, you have far more talent and resources than a Start-up. You are also clever enough to know that you do not have to reinvent the wheel or spend thousands of hours brainstorming new ideas. Just like the Chief Trending Officer idea, you can borrow ideas from other industries. You will be stunned by how many inspiring new thoughts are being implemented in other industries. How do you find these crazy new ideas? First, you must train your brain to look at unfamiliar trade magazine and blogs. We would even encourage you to start going to the wrong meetings. If you only go to accounting conventions, you are missing 99% of the world's most innovative practices. Try this. Get up early one Saturday morning. Drive to your nearest large hotel and walk into the lobby where they have erected that "Today's Meetings" board. Find a meeting you think you might enjoy. Be sure to dress well enough that your attire won't stand out as odd for a business meeting. Now with confidence, and your trusty note pad, walk into the wrong meeting. Don't freak out! You don't need an official badge. In fact, if anyone ever asks to see your badge, you look the person square in the eye and say, "I don't have a badge but I do want to sit in the meeting." 99.9% of the time they will assume it is their fault and escort you to an open seat. You will hear new trends, research, and business practices you've never heard before, all for free!

If, on the off chance they have hired security, and you can't get into the meeting, walk down the hall and slip into a different meeting.

Reward a Certain Amount of Failure

When I suggest that you come up with more ideas and innovations than a start-up, I am expecting that you will not have all of the execution details perfectly figured out. That's OK. In reality, there are no perfect companies. It's impossible. A free market economy is too evolutionary. You will always covet what your competitors have, and they will covet what you have. You will never get everything you want, when you want it. You will never be 100% relevant; and if you are, it will be temporary because circumstances are bound to change. Change is how you will maintain the agility of a Start-up. That's why we need to promote a culture that rewards fresh effort rather than complacency. Failure teaches you the lesson that you can't (and don't) know everything. Smart companies have an "Environment of Try." As I mentioned earlier, software companies and App developers launch imperfect "Beta" versions of their product because they know their first attempt probably isn't quite ready. Developers encourage user feedback and will send us updates; which is what we want. You and I accept that and we should encourage that attitude in our organizations.

Pitch Like This

If you have an idea you think will revolutionize your division or propel your company into the Fortune 100, here is how to launch your idea before your budget takes off on a wild goose chase.

1. Turn your idea into a written proposal. Having your ideas written down automatically lends more credibility than verbal spitballing. The document, to the

best of your knowledge and research, explains why your idea makes sense. Keep in mind that your idea needs to make money, save money, save time, and/ or increase effectiveness.

2. Give your "proposal" to a handful of people you respect who will give you honest feedback. This will allow you the chance to hear objections you may not have considered.

3. If you still want to advance your idea, ask your peers if they would support it. The purpose of getting buy-in from peers is so that you can go to the Boss with, "I've got something to show you. I think we have an opportunity to (insert your idea from above). I've got the support of Lorraine in Accounting and Sam in Sales."

4. When you make your presentation to the Boss, be confident and enthusiastic. Show the Boss you really care about this. Do your homework and give the Boss a projected R.O.I. Avoid using hyperbole and fantasy numbers. He or She will be appreciative of your realistic expectations.

5. If the Boss hedges with, "I just don't see it working." Ask for a low cost or no cost trial run. Say, "Can we at least see what our customers (i.e., clients, members, audience, shareholders, etc.) thinks of this? I'll make sure we stay under budget and I'll bring the raw numbers back to you in real time."

It will be very hard for the Boss to turn down a low risk exploratory test like that. Better yet, you will have demonstrated that you can perform your due diligence with wise analysis.

Why is Everybody Talking About Transparency?

I worked for a large company in the 1990's who was very controlling about anything the press department released. I was told, "We have a strict policy to hide the bad news." Rather hard to imagine that kind of thinking would still exist today but it does. Start-ups wouldn't think of hiding anything. They only know that bad news will eventually be discovered and they don't want to risk being vetted as liars. They know that 100% transparency (in good and bad times) will keep them out of trouble. I've been to some wonderful meetings where senior leaders admitted, "We've made a huge mistake and we apologize. We are correcting it and here are three things we're doing to do to make this better." Transparency fosters trust. While deception is hard to buy your way out of.

Bring Fun Back Into the Organization.

This is so simple I shouldn't have to say it. But I must.

Make it fun for people to come to work again. Say "Hello" to people when they come through the door. Smile at the people you work with like you're actually glad to see them. Do you think "instructing people to smile" is too elementary? Well then, you'll love this next story.

When I produced my first customer training film in 1995, I got a call from a mega retailer who had bought my film. But after previewing it, the HR director called me to say, "Ross, you didn't teach our people anything about smiling. You need to include a scene where you instruct people to smile at each other. And say something about smiling at the customer. Unless you tell them to do it, they just won't. We try to hire friendly people but they don't naturally smile at strangers."

Since then, I've never assumed people will automatically smile.

Look for ways to get together with people like a Start-up would. Institute company barbecues. Invite people to watch sporting events together. Have birthday parties and celebrate employee anniversaries and engagements. The only caveat is to make sure the event fits the vibe of your company culture. Here's an example of one that didn't. I went to an IBM post-meeting cocktail party and the music was deafening. The 55-year+ attendees didn't like the genre of music (Rap). The executives could only last a few minutes before vacating the party. By contrast, I went to a Hilton Worldwide conference that included a high-energy team-building event where everyone broke into groups and created new songs with famous songwriters. At Hilton they didn't want just a team-building event; they wanted to create friendships. Hilton included spouses and kids. You felt like it was a large family getting together for an ice cream social. There is a side benefit when you include the families at a company party. You reduce unnecessary and inappropriate sexual tension among your workforce.

Want more ideas?

Create a "company idol" competition where your people can lip sync their favorite tune. Conduct a fantasy sports team contest. Hold a "New Idea Harvest Day." Here's how it works. Each person who wants to submit a new idea pays five dollars to have their idea heard by the crowd. After all of the ideas have been pitched, a vote is taken and the best three ideas split the money. The prize money was the frosting on the cake but the various ideas made the meeting hilarious and engaging. Even though not every idea won a prize, it was clear that many of the other ideas would get folded into the company after the meeting.

Go "All In" With Social Media & Digital Marketing

This will sound like a broken record but your team must be uber-savvy about social media. All social media. This is where your Start-up competitors live so you better be comfortable with the neighborhood. If you aren't being proactively pursuing social selling, your team members will think you are completely out of touch with reality. They will wonder how long your company will last in the marketplace. We live in a recommendation economy and you cannot ignore social media as the engine that drives customer interaction.

What Social Media Will Make You Buzzworthy?

The Periscope APP is the something that can make you a star. Periscope has allowed Twitter account holders to do live broadcasts from anywhere. The best ones feature interesting places and events. "Interesting" being the key word. Don't just turn on your phone's camera and starting shooting something boring. As a guy who was a TV host and who did hundreds of man-on-the-street interviews, here are some tips to make your Periscope broadcasts attract more viewers.

Think of "Periscoping" as an adventure and you are our personal tour guide. Take your audience into a world they wouldn't normally get to see. The pace & energy should be brisk, not delivered in real time. What is real time? Professional broadcasters speak at between 180-220 words per minute (and viewers have no trouble keeping up). But in life, most people only speak at 120 words per minute; which can sound too sluggish for TV.

1. Prepare. It's always best to scout the location so you can plan your "story" and your "tour route." Ask yourself:

   "How is the lighting?" "Is natural (or artificial) lighting showing off our subject as we walk the route?"

   "How is the sound?" We don't want to lose awesome sound bites because the audience can't hear what is being said. Use a good clip-on microphone that connects directly into your iPhone, Galaxy, or Tablet.

2. Always use the horizontal camera view. The vertical angle is too restricting to a viewer who is used to watching movies or playing games on a flat screen TV, a computer monitor, or a tablet. The horizontal perspective will capture more ambience. The horizontal angle is also better when you upload to social media, YouTube, or your Website.

3. Can you surprise us along the route? If not, can we create some surprise guests or object to see?

4. "How should our tour end?" "What should we say or what should we promote as we end the piece?"

Viewers always remember the ending more than any other element of the tour. The ending is how your audience will judge their investment of time in watching you.

5. You're on the Air: Announce the reasons you are Periscoping (to reveal new items...to meet new people...to introduce a site not available to the public. i.e., "We are backstage at New York Fashion Week. Tickets are $500 but I'm going to take you deep inside the belly of this beast to show you what you can't see from the runway."

   Constantly "tease" your viewers about what you are doing – and what they will see next. TV shows are always telling us what is coming up next. "We have a celebrity here I want you to meet but I'm not going to tell you who it is yet. But, here is a clue. You will know her from TV and this is her home."

6. Appear to be spontaneous. We want the tour to feel unpredictable and authentic.... not contrived...so even though you have roughly planned your tour route, look for interesting people or locations along the way.

7. Invite viewers to participate. Your Twitter followers are watching this tour and can add likes and hearts during your show. Acknowledge them along the way.

"Hi Leah...glad you're joining us tonight."

"Bob, tell me what you like so far."

"Cameron is watching. Cam, did you see that last booth? Good idea, right?"

8. Wrap it up: Since this is the most important part of the tour it's Ok to 'stage' a finale. Maybe the final shot shows all the people in attendance...or reviews the most incredible spectacle of the tour. This is the time to reveal the person or object you have been teasing since the beginning.

9. Your Sign Off: Be sure to say, "Thank you for watching. I'm (your name). Don't forget to visit us at (give your website address) to see more."

10. Shoot and repeat...often.

Use Social Media to Intentionally Go Viral

We all want to scale our companies. So we can learn a lot from the Start-up campaigns that have gone viral (on a shoestring budget). Take the ALS Ice Bucket Challenge for example. ALS is the acronym for Amyotrophic Lateral Sclerosis, a progressive neurodegenerative disease that affects nerve cells in the brain and the spinal cord.

According to the ALS Association CEO, Barbara Newhouse, $220 million was raised worldwide. More than 17 million people participated in the challenge of dumping a bucket of ice on their heads. But why did the challenge go viral?

First of all, the cause was important. It was very easy for anyone to understand how to execute the challenge. You simply had to fill a bucket with household ice and be filmed dumping it on your head. Then, you challenged three of your friends to do the same. The brilliance of the challenge was that it had a 48-hour time limit. Your friends felt time pressure to meet the challenge. Since your friend challenged you personally, the element of a public dare was the key to participation.

What made it particularly interesting to me was that it wasn't a brand new idea.

The Ice Bucket Challenge wasn't dissimilar from the old "chain letters" we used to get as kids. Some of the letters promised a fortune would elude you if you broke the chain. Other letters threatened that if you didn't tell five friends and ask them to pass it on (within a certain time period) something bad would happen to you.

In this case, the challenge was fun and became cool when celebrities got into the action. The individual videos went viral on several different social media platforms. It didn't matter if you posted your challenge on Facebook, Tumblr, Twitter, Instagram, or any number of countless blog sites. The campaign was self-generating funny content. It was global marketing that cost absolutely nothing.

ALS enjoyed the public awareness and obvious financial rewards but the participants got something too. They felt socially responsible by doing something fun.

Dollar Shave Club is a Must See Viral Video

The viral video sensation created by this company didn't surprise anyone. The company sells multi-blade razors (for one dollar a month) on a subscription basis. Getting the word out on a totally new business model through conventional media could have cost millions. Instead, CEO Michael Dubin hired his friend and director Lucia Aniello. Dubin has a comedy background and came to her with a four page script. Aniello cut any script elements that weren't absolutely essential to the message and the humor. Since it was going to be posted on YouTube, they were not bound by the normal 30 or 60-second time restraints of TV or radio. Together they created a 1:34 video that was intentionally funny and edgy. Each frame and scene were carefully devised...even down to when Mike would drop the F-Bomb. ("Our blades are F***ing great!" In comedy, the joke is funny if the audience can't see the punch line coming and this video exploits that formula perfectly.

The proof was that within 48 hours, over 10,000 people signed up for the monthly delivery service. To date, more than 21,000,000 views have been logged on YouTube. Still haven't seen the video? Take a look. https://www.youtube.com/watch?v=ZUG9qYTJMsI

Win Awards and Get Famous

Top talent want to work for famous companies they can brag about to their friends. Growing up in Seattle, there was always a lot of pride if you could boast that you worked for Microsoft or Starbucks or The Seattle Seahawks. Getting press for winning awards (even industry awards) is a fast track for getting noticed by the talent you want. When you can legally say you are an award winning... (you name it) ... others are more likely to trust your work. It's proof that you have excelled at something.

Every year, Fortune Magazine rates the top 100 employers to work for. Why not find out what criteria is required to be considered? If you apply and win a spot in the top 100, the best eligible talent will conclude, "That company must be doing things right. They won the national award."

Besides winning a national award from Fortune, even an award within your industry will give you instant credibility. The fact is that if your industry thinks you are the best, others will feel confident about wanting to work for you. How awesome is that?

So how do you go about winning one of those awards?

First, you must decide you are going to submit your work for judging. Research how other companies won awards before you. What did they do? What categories did they enter? How did they attract attention? What did they do differently?

I am the Emcee for a lot of corporate and association ceremonies, so I'll tell you what I've seen. These winners delivered an outstanding achievement and/or performance. Often, they found an original point of view. A point of view that made their peers eyes bug out.

As a guy who has collected six television Emmy® awards, one Iris, and the National Speakers Association Hall of Fame award, I can tell you that those little statues have opened a lot of doors for me. I have earned more cash and contacts because of my "award winning" credibility than I ever would have achieved as a non-award winning schlub. If the award winners are moving ahead of you why don't you give it a calculated shot? Why don't you unseat them? At the very least, make them nervous that you've entered the competition.

Perk Up When You Recognize "The Perfect Storm"

Have you ever experienced the collision of timing and circumstance that caused your company to have almost exponential growth? I call it The Perfect Storm of enterprise. If you have been the benefactor of such an alignment, it probably caught you by complete surprise. Then, when you tried to repeat the phenomenon, nothing happened. Much of that fortunate confluence isn't something you can control. However, you can learn to watch for the signs that indicate circumstance and timing are about to collide so that you can jump on it sooner.

Make a Fad Popular Again

In my book, "Are You Relevant?" I wrote about a spectacular brand merchandise company called BDA Marketing in Seattle, Washington. (Benussen, Deutsch & Associates). Starting their business at 19 and 16 years-old respectively, Eric Benussen and Jay Deutsch began selling printed T-shirts at various Seattle events. They soon expanded to sell company-logo-specific T-shirts. Then, the boys were bold enough to ask the Seattle Seahawks if they could sell logo merchandise for them. At that time, NFL licensing was in the embryonic stage and BDA got the contract.

Always looking for new items to brand, Eric and Jay remembered how much they enjoyed the bobble head dachshund dogs that used to be perched in the back of a car's rear window. It occurred to them that nobody had thought to create sports-hero bobblehead dolls. Deutsche told me, "We thought the dolls would be popular but we didn't foresee the stampede. The press and lines of collectors formed around the stadiums because we had stumbled upon an instant fad. I guess you could say that what we did right was that we thought the dolls could be collectable. So, we only produced twenty-thousand units of each figure. Today you can find them on eBay for outrageous sums."

Since then, BDA has been expert at spotting trends before they went mainstream. Today, they routinely offer branded merchandise you didn't even know you needed until you saw it.

What Should You Look For?

Scan social media and mainstream press to spot emerging trends. Listen to what your friends are talking about. Pay attention to what they want. As I keep harping, it will be the public's appetite for your idea, your product, or your service that determines a runaway Perfect Storm success.

Think about what has happened with Fantasy Football. Millions of people love to assemble a fantasy team and create "clubs" with their friends. But the problem was that you had to wait until the season ended to get your payoff. Enter FanDuel and Draft Kings. These two companies made it possible for people to participate in the $40-70 billion dollar industry by creating a new team before every game. There is no season-long commitment and you get paid as soon as the game is over.

Abraham Lincoln said it best, "With public sentiment nothing can fail. Without it, nothing can succeed."

Louie, Louie for State Song?

I experienced such a public phenomenon during my first TV show was called, "Almost Live." It was a locally produced comedy/talk show on the Seattle NBC affiliate KING. We were given no marketing budget whatsoever. Therefore, any publicity was up to my cohorts and I. We worked diligently to come up with funny and innovative stunts to draw viewers to our upstart TV show.

Every idea flopped.

Even the publicity gags we loved were met with a lukewarm public response. Worse, our ratings were slipping.

Then, we landed on the notion to change the state song of Washington to "Louie, Louie."

Here's what happened.

I went on our weekly TV show and announced that we were going to lead a campaign to change the Washington State song from the unknown, "Washington My Home," to the rock hit, "Louie, Louie." The response went viral immediately. We couldn't print enough "Louie, Louie" buttons to keep up with demand. Newspapers wanted to cover the story. I even descended upon the state capitol in Olympia, Washington to plead with the state legislators, urging them to introduce official legislation.

Unwittingly, we'd hit a public nerve.

We planned to march on the capitol with our legion of supporters; which was pretty arrogant to think people would actually leave work to show up at the state capitol over a song.

We weren't prepared for the outcome.

Fifteen-thousand people showed up, during a workday, to support "Louie, Louie" as the new state song. Paul Revere and the Raiders set up on the capitol steps to play their version of the song. So did The Kingsmen (who made the song nationally famous) as well as The Wailers, a well known local band. Oh, and everyone in the news media also dropped by.

We were instantly famous. Our ratings doubled in the first 4 weeks. They doubled again within sixteen weeks. I was getting paid "appearance fees" to show up at corporate events, mall openings, and Christmas parties just to chat up the idea.

In some form or another, the "Louie, Louie" campaign was in the press for 211 straight days. We even got the Dubious Achievement Award from Esquire Magazine. A bona-fide phenomenon was taking place. Everywhere I went people wanted to know about the campaign.

TV icon, Dick Clark, had me as a guest on his national "Bloopers and Practical Jokes" TV show to talk about the Washington Capitol Rally. While we were never able to officially install "Louie Louie" as the state song, it is widely considered the unofficial state rock song.

Keep Your Head During a Phenomenon

As lucrative and flattering as all of that was, I didn't fall into the trap of thinking it was about me. I knew we'd hit a public vein. Also, just because you had a phenomenon once doesn't guarantee that it will happen again.

After our "Louie, Louie" success, I started getting offers to "consult" with advertising agencies who were looking for the next big thing in clothing, weed killers, automobiles; as if I had a crystal ball about such things. I had plenty of ideas but there was no way to predict their success.

In rare instances, you might have an opportunity to react to a situation that is considered an anomaly… something that doesn't happen very often (if ever). If you can identify the potential phenomenon and move quickly enough to capitalize on it, the "timing" of your reaction might turn into a spike in revenue or mass media attention. To outsiders, your swift action could be interpreted as "genius."

Treat People as...People

Legacy companies can not only become complacent about the business but also of people. We must remember that in a Start-up every person is a key contributor. Start-ups do not have extra money to motivate their teams so they rely on personal attention and pats on the back to keep the team performing at peak.

Legendary basketball coach Phil Jackson of the Chicago Bulls (and later the Los Angeles Lakers) had a similar philosophy. He was in the business of getting high performance from young, talented men who had wildly different upbringings. Yet Jackson's job was to get them all to collaborate with each other in the disciplined sport of basketball. Phil Jackson was successful because he knew each player was different and had a different perspective on their vision of success. When he first met each player he would give that person a book he knew they would enjoy. What is fascinating is that if you ask all the players to bring in their gift book from Coach Jackson, you would see that each player got a different book. Phil Jackson selected books he thought that individual player would like. And each player knew Phil Jackson cared about them individually as unique men, not just as a generic guy who could shoot a basketball.

Beware of Silo-ing

Whatever you do guard against creating silos. For the uninitiated the silo is that tightly bound department or business unit that protects itself from interference by the rest of the company. If you look at a farm silo there is one door at the bottom leading in and out. And the silo can only be reloaded from the top opening.

Breaking down the silos is not just a metaphor for that cylindrical Farm silo. Take a look at Apple's new headquarters in Cupertino, California. See how it is carefully designed for people to meet and greet in the middle as they pass each other from one area to another. Steve Jobs said it would be the ultimate collaborative workplace.

The Apple ring

A glimpse of Apple's new headquarters in Cupertino:

R&D space, laboratories

Two multilevel parking structures

Building is 4 stories, walled by curved glass, topped by solar panels

The circumference is about a mile; it takes 14 minutes to walk around

The diameter is about 1/3 of a mile

Wolfe Rd

Parking garage underneath ring

Cafeteria in 4-story atrium, indoor, outdoor seating

thousands of new trees include apple, apricot, olive, oaks

Source: Apple

BAY AREA NEWS GROUP

If you don't have the Apple-style ring, you can still position compatible departments adjacent to each other. Maybe your operations department needs to be closer to accounting. Or maybe your IT department needs to be adjacent to marketing, especially if you are engaged in a lot of digital marketing. Overall, personal relationships should rule your office geography.

Hire the Start-Up Mentality

This is where leadership can really shine. If you are dealing with complacent persons of responsibility, you'll want to talk to them about resurrecting that start-up mentality. If they can't, then an overhaul might be necessary. In which case you'll have an opportunity to find people who are driven again. Find innovative people and challenge them to motivate others. Set up competitive goals and situations that result in short-term quick wins. Be very careful not to onboard people who will say, "You know, I'm used to doing it the way we did in the big leagues." Anybody who comes into your organization with a swagger, predicated on their experience in the so-called big leagues, you must realize they could potentially cause dissension amongst those people who haven't played in that league. As a leader, it's your responsibility to manage humility over arrogance.

How About Re-thinking Your Org Chart?

Have you ever thought about redrawing your organizational chart like Dayton Freight did? As you can see, the customers are at the top. Senior leaders are at the bottom. You can imagine how a chart like that makes the typically lower level team members feel. In a word, important.

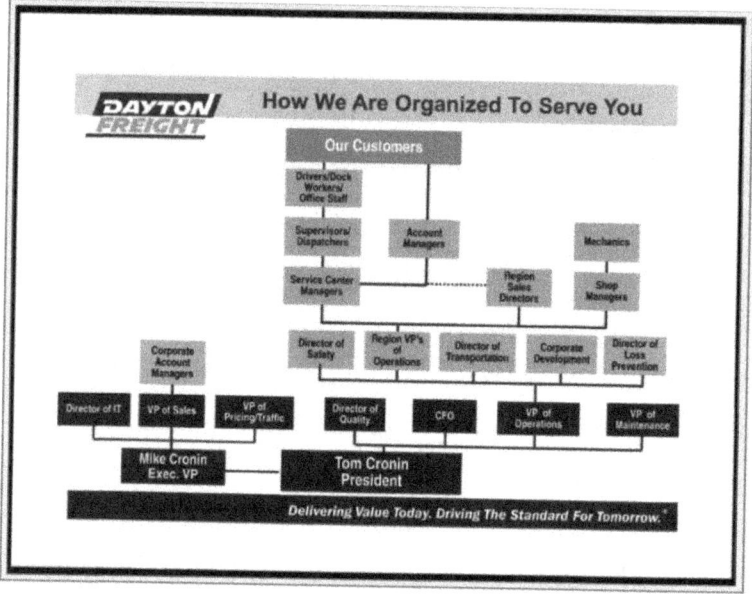

This Guy is My
"From-Legacy-to-Start-Up" Hero

We can all take a lesson from Alan Mulally, who took over Ford Motor Company in 2006. When Alan Mulally became the new CEO of Ford Motor Company he said, "We have been going out of business for forty years." And, he was right. A succession of ineffective Ford family members had put their company in the bullseye of bankruptcy to the tune of $24 billion. Mulally, who had spent his entire 37-year career at Boeing Aircraft, not only erased the debt (in eight years) but he made Ford a world beater again. But how did he do what generations of Ford relatives couldn't? First, he had to squash the stigma that he didn't know the car business. Long time Ford executives quizzed him, "How are you going to tackle something as complex and unfamiliar as the auto business when we are in such tough financial shape?" Mulally responded, "An automobile has about 10,000 moving parts, right? An airplane has two million, and it has to stay up in the air."

End of discussion.

Like the phrase from a past Ford marketing campaign, Mulally knew that "Job One" was to get Ford off financial life-support. He arranged to have Ford borrow $23.6 billion by mortgaging all of Ford's assets. When the US Government held bailout hearings to American Automobile Manufacturers, Ford was the only member of the "Detroit Three" who didn't take a loan. And when Mulally and other industry leaders were criticized for flying to the hearings in their private jets, Mulally sold all but one of Ford's private jets and started road-tripping from Detroit to Washington in a Ford-built hybrid electric vehicle. Mulally then did what many insiders thought was the unthinkable. He suspended dividends to shareholders.

Back in Detroit, Mulally had to get every worker to believe in "The Way Forward." He executed a restructuring plan through positive servant leadership. His personal humility rallied the assembly line, the IT department, the middle managers, and the Board of Directors. He was able to convince everyone that there is always a way forward, and that he could be trusted to lead the team. He had continually reinforced the idea that everyone is part of the team and each person's contribution is respected and valued; therefore, everyone should participate in reaching the goal. Each employee was given a card to carry with them that detailed the business plan on one side, and the culture and expected behaviors on the other.

Mulally also listened to their ideas.

In the old days of Ford, if an employee saw a problem and stopped production, a manager would have jumped down their throat and questioned their judgment. Under Mulally, managers were retrained to explore the problem and work with the employee to resolve it.

Mulally got executives to re-imagine the future of Ford by waging war games. He encouraged every employee to see Ford not simply as a car company, but as a "mobility company." Mulally was changing the internal culture and fostering collaboration. He built a workplace where innovation began to flourish.

Mulally became well-known for reeling in labor costs. In 2008, Mulally achieved what many believed to be impossible by negotiating four new agreements with the United Automobile Workers, which brought down labor costs from $76/hour to $55/hour.

The company saw its first profitable quarter in over two years.

When anyone asks about his "servant" leadership style Mulally says,"At the most fundamental level, it is an honor to serve — at whatever type or size of organization you are privileged to lead, whether it is a for-profit or nonprofit. It is an honor to serve. Starting from that foundation, it is important to have a compelling vision and a comprehensive plan."

Mulally left the company in 2014 with a legacy that fueled Ford Motor Company to go from a record multibillion-dollar loss in 2006 — to five consecutive years of annual profits. But this isn't just a story about making money. When he came to Ford, Mulally may not have known the car business, but he knew how to inspire people to believe they could achieve greatness from their ideas — not just by a command and control directive from the Boss.

Mulally made Ford a safe place to bring up problems. So can you. Encourage people. Be humble in asking for their help. Allow them to bring up problems in a culture that doesn't relegate them to the penalty box.

Be a Workplace That Offers Access to the Future

Think about what the future will look like. The oldest Millennials will be 40 years-old by the year 2020 and ready to take over your company. These "digital natives" grew up installing home routers and building websites for their parents. Millennials made Facebook and Twitter rich. So, by 2020 they will expect technology to start working for them, 24/7/365.

The workday in 2020 will begin with auto-synchronization of a team member's laptop, iPad, smart watch, tablet, and wearable connected clothing; all of which will be displayed on the 17" dashboard monitor of their "connected" self-driving car. The monitor will alert them where to go for their appointments. When they arrive at a GPS-enabled office building, an elevator bay will welcome them (by name) for a ride to their preprogrammed floor...and of course, if there are any changes in the schedule or meeting space, digital push notices will be sent to all meeting attendees via smart re-sync. During the meeting (either teleconference or live), management will be apprised of who attended the meeting and each contributor's data will be logged; in Real-Time. In fact, Real-Time will replace forensic (historical) responses because social listening software will be collecting and analyzing millions of incoming comments and suggestions instantly. These comments will be categorized and rated as to their emotionality so that leaders can examine trending data like, "Poor supply chain results are trending at XYZ Company and 43% of females responded in an angry tone." That's Real-Time data collection.

However, the most important conversations will revolve around predictive trends and outcomes. "Smart Bots" will be scanning the cultural landscape looking for shifting buying habits and competitors hiding in your blind spot.

Of course, management of all this data collection and trend analysis sounds like a huge time-sucker, right? Relax. Each team member will have their own Social Avatar (personal artificial-intelligence engine) working over the weekend gathering case studies, comparing process and cost analysis, making risk assessments and creating financial feasibility models. While your co-worker was attending a child's soccer game, his or her Social Avatar was busy preparing recommendations for your Monday meeting; based on your company's fiscally-safe predetermined parameters. Fact-based decision-making will replace "gut feelings."

This isn't fantasy.

These technologies already exist and the infrastructure for such magic is quickly being installed at a company near you. Full inculcation is only five years away...Yikes!

Will you be ready? If not, I'd be happy to help you prepare.

TO CONTACT ROSS SHAFER

Please visit: www.RossShafer.com

Phone: (910) 256-3495

Email: Helen@RossShafer.com

ABOUT ROSS SHAFER

 Ross Shafer is one of America's most no-nonsense thought leaders on motivating change, customer experience, enterprise growth, and market relevance.

In this book, Ross weighs in on the tactics he feels are necessary for personal success and career growth.

As a former college football linebacker and serial-re-inventor, Ross has been self employed since the age of 23. His first business was a stereo and pet shop on the Puyallup, Washington Indian reservation. From there he began a career as a small business turnaround artist. As a sideline, Ross became an accomplished stand up comedian who transitioned to a successful TV hosting and producing run that found him competing against late night television icon, David Letterman. Ross earned six Emmy Awards in the process. Ross has since returned to his business roots where he has been consumed with the study of how cultural changes cause some organizations to experience wild success while others disappear into extinction.

OTHER BOOKS BY ROSS SHAFER

Nobody Moved Your Cheese
(How to Ignore the Experts and Trust Your Gut)

Are You Relevant?
(12 Reasons Smart Organizations Thrive in Any Economy)

The Customer Shouts Back
(How to Create Lifelong Customers)

Grab More Market Share
(How to Wrangle Business Away From Lazy Competitors)

Customer Empathy
(Stories of Internal and External Customer Service)

Absolutely Necessary
(Bulletproof Tactics That Will Put You in High Demand)